THE PRAYER COTTAGE

and the

SACRED GARDEN

THE PRAYER COTTAGE

and the

SACRED GARDEN

Experiencing Intimacy with Christ

Rocky Fleming

ROCKY FLEMING

Published by Prayer Cottage Publications
Rogers, Arkansas

Scripture taken from the New American Standard Bible®,
Copyright © The Lockman Foundation 1995.

ISBN 0-9742383-0-9

Manufactured in the United States of America

CONTENTS

Come to Me, all you who labor and are burdened,
and I will give you rest.
Take My yoke upon you and learn from Me,
for I am meek and humble of heart,
and you will find rest for yourselves.
For My yoke is easy, and My burden light.

— *Jesus Christ*

ONE

The Prayer Cottage

You've been there before—to that place in life where nothing seems to work out without a fight. All your projects, even labors of love, present monumental challenges. Your family and friends take a beating because of the tension that permeates your life. No matter what you do, you can't find peace with yourself.

For weeks I had been living in just such a season, and for no apparent reason. Every aspect of my life was in place just as I had planned and hoped that it would be. And yet, something was missing; that's the only way to describe it. I felt a deep longing within my soul that could not be satisfied with the life that I had worked so hard to attain. I had everything I had ever thought I would need to experience happiness: a beautiful wife and precious children, a great job, money in the bank, and my retirement secure. Just about anything I had wanted to experience in life, I had been able to do. I had, at that time, what my friends described as "the dream life." But the life I displayed to others was an illusion, for inside I was hollow and troubled. They never saw the fears that troubled me and the controlled rage that I kept hidden from their view. Something, and I had no idea what it could have been, was eating me up inside.

Things came to a head after a particularly disappointing sales meeting. I had been working on a make-or-break case for several months, but in the midst of my presentation, I couldn't stay focused. My mind kept wandering away from the meeting and the questions being asked of me. Never before had I needed to be excused from such an important meeting, but I just had to leave. So I asked my customers if they would excuse me. Thank goodness they knew me well enough to know that my behavior was out of character, and we rescheduled the meeting for another time. Afterward I made arrangements to spend the weekend alone at a friend's mountainside cabin. Some time away, I hoped, would allow me to refocus.

It was the year that the Hale-Bopp comet passed close enough to Earth that anyone could spend hours viewing its spectacular trek across the nighttime skies. Like most other things, I hadn't given myself any time to see the beautiful comet that everyone else was talking about. It was something I had in mind to do that weekend at the cabin, along with trying to find some answers to my troubles.

After getting settled in the small cabin, I made my way to the front porch, which overlooked a valley and had an unobstructed view of the eastern sky. At first glance the comet was impressive, with its point of light and tail rising above it. But as my eyes became more adjusted to the dark, I saw even more of the tail, which, after a few minutes, appeared as a faint streak halfway across the sky. It takes a lot to impress me, but I was awed by the spectacular sight. That comet was nothing but a frozen ball of rock that spent most of its life floating dark and cold through the space. Then for a short while it passed so close to the sun that it glowed white and threw off its brilliant tail.

I stared up at the visitor to our solar system as I settled back in my chair on the porch and began to think through my day, and then about my own life's journey. My mind wandered back to certain events in my lifetime that had marked both my progression in life and the key change points that led to my life as it was that day.

I thought about the young boy who always needed to prove his value to himself and to others—how I would challenge myself with games or daredevil tricks, just to see if I could accomplish them. I thought about the young man who kept his nose to the grindstone in everything he attempted for fear of failure and disapproval by the people around him. I thought of the rigidly disciplined man who had developed over the years—how I rarely cut much slack for others, and even less for myself.

I knew that a "panther" in me had been created in the early years that had helped me claw through life and achieve success in everything I put my mind to. He had served me well for fifty years. But he was no longer my friend. He was no longer serving his master. He had now turned on me and was eating me up inside.

As I stared up at that comet, I realized that I, too, was hurtling through life as lonely and cold as it was. At some point in my life I had been close enough to God's light to capture His glow, but now I was so far from His light, I wondered if there was any glow left in me.

I stared into the darkness and I prayed, "God, where are You?"

I had heard others speak of an indescribable peace that could be found in a special time with the Savior, but it had eluded me. I had received Jesus Christ as my Savior many years before, but I hadn't found that intimacy that some people claim when they speak of Him. I was beginning to think that this intimacy with Jesus that they were talking about was either a result of an overworked imagination or it was given only to a few people. Either way, I hadn't experienced it.

I had always approached my prayer time and spiritual

life much like my business: It was something that needed to be taken care of, a priority, and I would just have to do it. However, unlike my other business and life interests, I often charged into my prayer time without any thought or preparation. As a result, I found myself mouthing words I had heard myself say many times before. Eventually the dreaded condition of "rote" entered my life. My words were good and heartfelt, but they lacked the intimacy that two friends enjoy with their conversation, and I knew it.

Somehow I knew that the Lord was glad I was praying, but I also knew something wasn't as it should be, and I was missing out. He was trying to break through to me and whisper words of encouragement that would calm my fears and even give me the answers I was seeking. But something kept me busy, agitated, impatient, and even deaf to His words. I knew enough about the dynamics of obvious sin and disobedience in a life and how that can break fellowship with the Lord. But I couldn't find any of those particular things in my life. I was disheartened by my frustration with life. As I sat on the porch watching that comet, I knew that if I didn't change my life's direction, I soon would find myself so deep in the dark night of space I would never find my way back again. I was frightened.

I bowed my head and cried out, "Father, please help me! I'm falling apart. I can't go on like this any longer. I am spiritually anemic and dying inside, and I'm desperate for You to show me what is wrong in my life."

I slumped over, held my head in my hands, and remained silent. A gentle breeze blew across the back of my neck. In the distance I could hear a dog bark and a child cry from a house in the valley below. I stayed in this position for a long time. Just before rising to go inside the cabin, I heard a soft whisper spoken directly to my inner being.

"My child, come to My Sacred Garden," the voice whispered, "and I will give you the peace you want."

I didn't know what to think of the voice I had just heard. So I waited quietly to see if my imagination was playing tricks on me. Then I heard the whisper again.

"My child, come to My Sacred Garden."

Hesitantly I asked, "Who is speaking to me?"

"It is He that you are seeking," the voice replied.

Maybe it was my desperation that made me respond as I did, but I had no doubt that it was the Lord speaking to me. I realized that He had responded to my plea and had broken through to me. My walls of self-sufficiency had fallen down, and maybe this was what He was waiting for. He offered me an invitation to His Sacred Garden, so I responded, "Lord, what is the Sacred Garden?"

"It is a special place where we are able to have fellowship unlike anything you have experienced before," He whispered.

"Will You take me there?" I asked.

He answered, "Yes, I will, but you must first proceed through the Prayer Cottage."

"What is the Prayer Cottage?"

"You will see."

I closed my eyes and tried to make sense of what had just happened. As I did, I began to drop off and lose consciousness, although it was different from going to sleep. I felt like I was falling through space, being carried to some place far from my chair. It was a strange awareness, for I knew that my body was still on the cabin porch, but my conscious mind was as sharp and cognizant as ever.

Then suddenly, I no longer had the falling sensation. I felt like I had stopped traveling. I slowly opened my eyes and I could see that I was now in a new place. As I looked at my new surroundings, I felt like I was in a fog. Then the fog began to clear and a beautiful old cottage came to my view.

The cottage looked similar to paintings I had seen before but with its own unique features. It had a steep, thatched roof and a chimney from which smoke was rising. The front yard was bordered by a picket fence with wild roses climbing though the slats. A high privacy hedge touched the sides of the cottage near the back and enclosed the area behind the cottage. From the trees that I could see standing tall over the hedges, I knew that a special place, hidden from my view, must lie behind the cottage.

As I approached the cottage and ascended the wooden steps that led to the protected stoop, I saw that the front door was open. I stood before the door and heard my Savior inside the house say, "Come into the front room and I will guide you through the house."

Two

The Grace Room

As I entered the door into the front room of the cottage, I heard the Lord's voice say, "I call this room the Grace Room."

"Why is that, Lord?" I responded.

"I call it the Grace Room because I put no conditions on those who come into it. I have heard people say they will come to Me when they get their life straightened out. As a result, many stay away from Me, struggling with habits and choices they can't control. They think I won't love them unless they are lovable. But I wish they knew that everyone has to enter into a relationship with Me through My grace, and My grace welcomes all. Even the best people can't be good enough to approach Me through their works, and even the worst people are welcome through My grace."

The Lord continued, "My children do not understand that it is the same with the sanctified life. To abide with

Me comes not by busyness and good deeds, but rather by the provision that I have made for them to have intimacy with Me."

"Lord," I asked, "what is the provision for intimacy with You? You are my Savior, but I am not aware of this provision."

"You will understand as you proceed," the Lord answered. "In prayer I want My children always to feel welcome and to come to Me no matter what the condition of their lives. But I also want them never to forget that it is by My grace that the invitation always stands and the process begins. I want you always to keep My grace in your mind when you approach Me. Just as My grace was essential for your first step to Me when you responded to My salvation invitation, it is also necessary that the first room in the Prayer Cottage is the Grace Room."

"Lord," I said, "I understand this. I've been learning about and singing about your 'amazing grace' since I was a child."

"No my child," the Lord continued, "you do not understand. You have a head knowledge of My grace, but you do not have a heart knowledge. Your empty life and your lack of joy testifies to this truth about you. But you asked for My help. This is good. You are aware of an emptiness within you, and you have beseeched Me in earnest. Therefore, as I have promised, You have found Me, and I will reveal to you the source of the disturbance that is within your soul and what must be done to expel it."

These words both comforted and encouraged me.

The Lord then said, "In the Grace Room I want you to slow down and consider My grace. I don't want a liturgical confession of faith about My grace, as you often do in a church service. I want you instead to remember the pitiful conditions that I have removed you from in times past. I want you to think about the things for which I have forgiven you and the great price I paid in order to redeem you so that you could have the relationship you desire with Me. Most of all, I want you to think of what My grace means to you as you approach Me with your prayers. Child, I desire your heart and not your words as you reflect on My grace."

After listening to the Lord's words preparing me for what was next, I looked around the Grace Room. My eyes were drawn to a comfortable, overstuffed chair, the only furniture in the room. The chair was placed by a fireplace, where a warm, crackling fire was burning. On the walls I saw pictures of my family and friends, snapshots of my life's most enjoyable moments. "Stay here," my Savior said. "Rest in My grace before you go farther into the Prayer Cottage."

I settled into the chair and immediately felt its loving acceptance. I breathed out a weary sigh, and a wonderful calmness fell over me. I was leaving behind all the problems that were with me before I entered this room. I felt that God was giving me permission to not think about deadlines, commitments, and troubles for the time being.

As I enjoyed that simple reprieve and the warmth of God's fire that He had prepared for me, I remembered that my Savior wanted me to think about His unconditional love and what that grace means to me when I approach Him in my prayer time. It was apparent that He sees this reflection as important in preparing my heart for prayer.

I looked at the pictures on the wall and was reminded of how blessed I was with the treasures of my family and friends. The pictures reminded me of some of my most special times with them. I could not help but be reminded, as I lingered in the Grace Room, that I had never accomplished anything that warranted His love and blessings. God's grace and Jesus' sacrifice was the only thing that had granted me entrance into His family and the benefits of being His child. Then it began to dawn on me that this was the purpose of the Grace Room, to prepare me for meeting with the Savior. When I remembered His grace and mercy to me, a spirit of thankfulness began to permeate my soul. I could now see that a grateful heart and a thankful attitude are necessary conditions for moving closer to the Lord. I could also see that this had been missing in my prayer life, and I had never adequately prepared for my time with Him. The memories of His forgiveness to me also began to have a strange effect on some of the negative feelings I had about other people. The realization of His grace was softening my heart. In this state of thankfulness for my own forgiveness, another thought began to emerge. I could sense that this thought was preparing me for what was next. Then I heard Him calling me. So I ventured into the next room in the Prayer Cottage.

THREE

The Examination Room

Through an open door I heard the Lord call, "My child, come into the next room." As I stepped through the door, He said, "I call this the Examination Room." The room was stark and white, somewhat like a surgical room in a hospital but without all the machinery. I wondered why the Examination Room was so sterile and cold, especially after leaving the comfort of the Grace Room. I asked the Lord to explain.

"Because you are entering a very serious condition of prayer, which is self-examination," came the answer. "My child, true repentance comes as a result of a painful examination of your life. In your self-examination, sins that you've hidden from your own consciousness are exposed to you. In this room you ask Me to help you see areas of your life that are wrong in My sight, and I reveal them to you. When I reveal these things, I want you to lay them before Me and repent. This means you come to an agreement with Me that certain things are sins in your life and that you need My help with them. When that happens, you and I can get down to business of how to overcome the temptation you will face to repeat that sin."

"Lord, why is self-examination necessary?" I asked. "Why can't we just be aware of our sin and seek Your forgiveness?"

The Lord answered, "As you spend more time with Me and in My Word, you will become more aware of the things I am opposed to. However, the basic nature of the human is to hide. People try to hide sin from Me, which is impossible. But in their attempt to hide sin from Me, they deceive themselves. They take the seriousness of their sin lightly. Only if they are caught do they seem to regret what they have done.

"They come to Me and tell Me something is wrong in their life. They ask Me for new jobs, new spouses, or healing from their depression as an antidote for their pain. They ask Me to snap My fingers and give them the joy that they read about or see in others, but they don't want to look at the root problem that has created their misery. They've been so sure of their self-righteousness, they are unwilling to consider the condition in their life that keeps Me from being able to bless them. Their self-deception has literally blinded them to their sin. If they only knew that I want to give all My children the desires of their heart. But I tell you, as long as there is a condition of pride or unrepentance, and as long as their hearts are not after Me, I will not remove them from their miserable conditions. Instead, I will leave them in their misery until they examine themselves, repent of their sin, and return to Me. Self-examination is painful but necessary."

As I listened, I couldn't help but realize that something was wrong in my own life, for it was out of frustration that I had entered the Prayer Cottage in the first place. I understood that my Savior had brought me to this room so that He could bless me, but right now I had to look inward and find out what was wrong in my life.

"Savior," I said, "I feel that I need some time to examine myself."

"Call Me when you are ready," He said.

I folded my hands behind my back and began pacing slowly through the Examination Room. The room wasn't big, nor was it cluttered with furniture, so I was in no danger of running into anything as I closed my eyes. With no clues in the room like the images on the wall of the Grace Room, I wasn't sure where to begin self-examination. I asked, "Lord, show me areas of my life that are offensive to You. I know something is wrong, but I don't know what it is. I need Your help to see the problem."

At first nothing happened, so I waited quietly. Suddenly, images of ugly and despicable things I had done flashed before my eyes. Other people had seen some of those things, but only my Savior and I knew most of the sins. Therefore, I knew that there must be a reason that He was bringing those sins to my mind. As the pictures floated through my mind, a creeping remorse began to invade my thoughts. Before the remorse could find its lodging, another picture floated into my view saying, "Forgiven and removed from My memory!" This brought relief and joy, as I remembered how I originally felt when Jesus forgave me of those sins.

I continued to wait. Slowly a thought began to emerge, as I recollected from the deep recesses of my mind memories of unresolved anger, bitterness, and resentment. These memories were still there because some individual who had hurt me had never asked for my forgiveness and, as a result, I had never resolved the matter. I had felt justified in keeping my memories of those wrongs in an unforgiven status, because I just didn't feel that the people who hurt me deserved my forgiveness, and, furthermore, they had never asked for it. It didn't matter that the incidents had happened years before, that the persons didn't know they had hurt me, or even that some of them were dead. I just knew that as long as I kept the memory of their offense alive, I was somehow getting even with them.

As I evaluated my reasons for the memories, a vision

of a justice scale like the one displayed in a court of law appeared. One end of the scale was heavily tipped, showing an obvious weight difference in the trays. I looked more closely and saw a sign on the heavily weighted side. It said, "Your sins against Me." On the side of the scale that carried the lighter weight, a sign read, "Their sins against you."

As I considered the comparison, I heard my Savior say, "Do you need My justice or My grace when it comes to your sins against Me?" Without waiting for my answer, He continued, "Do they need your justice or your grace with their sins against you?"

The searing truth of the question made me realize that my unresolved anger, which had never given me peace, resulted from the standard of justice I demanded of others. The unforgiveness I felt toward these people was as ugly as any sin I had ever committed. It was a spiritual cancer that had lodged deep within my soul and had found justification for being there. Like any cancer that eventually consumes the host, mine was destroying my joy, my spiritual health, and my intimacy with my Savior. My spiritual cancer of unforgiveness had been exposed.

I had taken lightly my Savior's teaching in Matthew 6 about my own forgiveness when He said, "For if you forgive men for their transgressions, your Heavenly Father will also forgive you. But if you do not forgive men, then your Father will not forgive your transgressions."

The reality of the scales of justice still loomed before me, and I could see that if I had been judged according to the standard that I demanded of those who had hurt me, I would be found guilty. I needed my Savior's grace, for if given justice, I could never deserve His forgiveness and pardon. I would be desperately lost and without any hope.

In the Grace Room I had begun to realize the dynamics of my Savior's grace and how that grace is necessary in all aspects of my relationship with Him. I was now seeing that I must convey my own unconditional forgiveness to others, especially to those whom I didn't think deserved it. In the Examination Room I now understood that my greater concern should be my sin of unforgiveness and how it hurt my intimacy with my Savior. The hurt that I had inflicted on myself because of unforgiveness was far greater than anything that people had done to me. My unforgiveness was keeping my Savior from blessing me. The painful truth, I now realized, was that I could be missing out on the desires of my heart simply because of my stubborn, prideful sin of unforgiveness.

A cold sweat began to slide down the back of my neck. The Examination Room had effectively revealed something awful in my life that I had hidden from myself. I thought again about the many things God had done for me, out of no other motivation than His gracious love. Like a Times

Square neon sign, the words *Grace or Justice? Grace or Justice?* flashed before my eyes. As my heart raced, a strange desire began to stir. I wanted to run to God and ask Him to bless those persons who had sinned against me.

In the stark reality of my self-examination, I knew that forgiveness, like He wanted, had made its way to my heart. I realized that I didn't want God's vengeance on those people but rather His blessing for them. I now saw them as victims rather than culprits, and I wanted them to have their eyes opened to my Savior's gracious love. I just couldn't hold my feelings back, and I found myself saying, "Lord, forgive me for holding those things against these people. I forgive them, and I ask You to forgive them, as well. Please, My Lord, don't hold what they've done to me against them. Instead, bless them and all that is in their lives. Open their eyes to Your love so they will know You as I do. I feel so ashamed that I haven't seen these situations through your eyes and I have kept this unforgiveness in me. Please forgive me, Lord. I am desperate without Your grace, just like they are. I agree with You, Savior. This is a sin in my life. I need Your forgiveness and Your help to remove all my anger against these people. I've been blind, but now I see."

As I began to regain awareness of the Examination Room, it became apparent that my Savior had led me to understand that this room is a place for taking stock of my life and finding out what things offend God. I was made aware that with this and any other sin, my fellowship with my Savior would be obstructed if I didn't come to repentance. The time I spent in this room was demanding. It was a time of spiritual surgery, and it was hard but necessary. It had drained me. I was covered with sweat and tears and felt dirty with my sin. As I lay in the stain of my exposed sin, I heard my Savior say, "Now, come to the Courtyard, but leave your dirty garments here."

FOUR

The Courtyard

I have been to many wonderful spas throughout the world, but none of them could compare with what I was now seeing. As I stepped through the door leading from the Examination Room, I entered an inner courtyard leading from The Prayer Cottage. The courtyard was filled with many varieties of fragrant plants. In the center of the courtyard was a boulder that rose over thirty feet. Crystal clear water gurgled from the top of the boulder and cascaded down its side. About halfway down the rock, a protrusion forced the water outward and created a waterfall, which fell into a pool and ran off down a rocky brook.

I heard my Savior say, "My child, your sins are forgiven and are removed from you as far as the east is from the west. Wash and linger here a while. I will be waiting for you in the Sacred Garden when you are ready."

A sigh of relief escaped me when I heard my Savior

tell me that He forgave me. Even though I know that He is a God of grace, I also know He takes sin very seriously. I knew I could never take His grace for granted again, and the justified fear that was within me was a sobriety check on that conviction. I was also drained and a little chilled from my Examination Room experience. I stepped under the waterfall and let its waters flow upon me. When the water hit me, it was warm and gentle. My body began to relax as the salt crust of tears and perspiration was washed away. It was just like my Savior to look at all my needs. He knew I needed this affirmation of His forgiveness, and this bath symbolized His cleansing of my sin and its results.

As I stepped from the waterfall and the pool, I noticed that a gleaming white robe had been placed on a rock next to the pool. I wrapped the robe around me. The scent of the fresh, clean garment was the same as the fragrance of the rest of the courtyard.

I was feeling a strange depletion, but without the emptiness that I had experienced before entering the Prayer Cottage. It was if a great load I had been carrying for a long time had been lifted from me and I suddenly realized how weary I had been. I still felt weak from the experience and needed more rest before going farther. My Savior said for me to linger a while in the Courtyard. So I rested on a patch of grass near the waterfall.

As I lay my head back on the grass and let the sound

of the water soothe me, I began to be refreshed. I was reminded that Jesus spoke of Himself in terms of being "Living Water" to the tired and the thirsty. I realized that He wasn't speaking of a thirst in the body, but rather a thirst in the soul. I had no idea how spiritually thirsty I had been until I began to see what I had been missing.

I remembered His words of forgiveness and how He said that my sin was completely removed from me. Before entering the Cottage, I don't think I really understood the depth and completeness of God's forgiveness. The thought came to me that this is why I have a hard time forgiving myself. I've consistently seen it in others and myself. For some reason our healthy repentance turns unhealthy when we continue beating ourselves up over our failure. We just can't believe that God can thoroughly forget our sin, so we have to keep proving to Him that we are sorry by not forgiving ourselves. I could see why my Savior wanted me to understand His grace better at the beginning of this vision journey, for His grace gives me complete freedom from living with guilt and shame. His grace not only forgives me, but it also empowers me with a pure desire to live out my life as one who has been forgiven. I no longer see it as something that I need to prove to God, but rather an opportunity to live out my gratitude before people and before Him.

I was beginning to feel my strength return to me and

a renewed interest to continue my journey to the Sacred Garden. I rose from my patch of grass and noticed a path beside the rocky brook leading out of the Courtyard. I followed it to see where it would lead.

FIVE

The Sacred Garden

The transition from The Courtyard to the breathtaking grove of fruit trees, shrubs, and flowers was subtle. I could see that I was entering a new area as I passed through the arch of roses that wove through the trellis over the path. When I passed under the trellis, I was overwhelmed with a sense of awe. I had come to a holy place like none that I had seen before. The painful preparation I had been through was well worth the time, the tears, and every bead of sweat. I shook my head as I asked myself, "Why have I kept myself from this blessing?" My Savior had invited me into His Sacred Garden, and everything I had experienced had prepared me for it. Never had I felt so ready to meet with Him. I was clean and fresh. I had a new song in my heart that wanted to sing praises and thankfulness to my Savior. I was ready to worship Him.

"Welcome, My child, to My Sacred Garden," I heard

my Savior say. "This is a place where My children and I do our best communicating. In this place poetry, songs, and inspired words are written. Here I am able to impart My wisdom to those who seek it. Here all concerns are brought to Me and burdens are lifted from the weary soul that has truly sought My help. Here My children are able to hear from My own mouth words that say I love them and have special plans for them."

"Savior," I said, "I can't find words that are worthy of You. I want to sing Your praise, bring You my love, and give to You the thankfulness I feel. But I feel woefully inadequate."

"My child, I see your heart, and that is enough for me." He continued. "The Holy Spirit, right this minute, is speaking heavenly words to Me that are from your heart. He is translating your deep feelings for Me into heavenly words of praise. My throne room is being bathed with the fragrance of your thanksgiving and worship."

I was about to weep with this last comment, but before I did, I heard my Savior say, "Come and walk with Me in My garden. I have some things to show you."

As I strolled down the path that followed the rocky stream, I was surrounded by unfamiliar trees and fruit. Every tree was loaded with fruit. They appeared to be ripe and ready to be picked, but all remained on the tree. I asked, "Savior, I've never seen trees or fruit like these before. What are their names?"

"You will never see anything like this fruit in your world," He said. "These can be grown only in My kingdom. As far as their names go, they are heavenly names, and I will have to translate their names for you. Before I do, take a bite and taste some of the fruit."

I picked one of the dangling fruits. It was about the size of a large grapefruit, but that was all that was the same. The thin skin of the fruit was smooth and cool. It was soft, yet firm. I bit into the fruit. Immediately an explosion of flavor filled my mouth. The fruit's juices ran down the sides of my mouth and dripped from my chin. A strange joy filled my soul. I didn't think my emotions could soar any higher, but they had now moved to a higher peak.

"Wow," I said. "What is the name of this one?"

"That particular fruit, translated into your words, is called Joy," the Lord answered.

I could understand this, for I was feeling joy like never before.

"What about those?" I asked, pointing to several other varieties.

"That one is called Love, the other, Peace, and there is Patience. Behind that tree is Self-Control, behind it is Kindness. You will also find some other kinds of fruit farther in the Garden," He answered.

I remembered reading in the Bible that the fruits of

the Spirit are "love, joy, peace, patience, kindness, good-ness, faithfulness, gentleness, and self-control." I was get-ting a better understanding that the fruits mentioned in Galatians 5 are something supernatural and can come only from my Savior.

The Lord continued, "These are the fruits that my chil-dren partake of when they come to My garden and abide with Me. They are also My characteristics that are expressed in the life of one who abides with Me. Many other fruits in My garden are provided for special occasions. For instance, if special words are needed to encourage someone, I have fruit for that. Or, if a particular person requires extra un-derstanding, I will provide that fruit for My child to give to that person. You name it, and I have a provision for My child. But come, let me show you around. There will be other times that I can give to you a more thorough under-standing. Right now, I want to show you what you can experience with Me when you come to My Sacred Garden."

For a long while we walked through the garden. He showed me special places where I could sit and talk to Him. These special places all had names and were dedi-cated for a specified prayer emphasis. He led me to each prayer station and taught me how I could sit with Him and pray. These are the places He took me:

SIX

The Intercession Bench

The Lord led me first to a bench in the Garden. I sat on it as He began to speak.

"My child, this is a dedicated place in the Sacred Garden that I want you to meet with Me and bring to me names of people that you have concern for. It is called the Intercession Bench."

After a pause, He continued, "I want you to ask My help for these people. When you bring to Me these people and their needs, I will either help them directly or give you the wisdom to know how you can help them."

"Savior," I said, "I often struggle with prayer in this area; I just don't know what to ask for and what they truly need."

He replied, "You do not have to know all of their needs or any of their needs at all to bring them to Me. Understand this: Foremost is the delight I feel when I see My children concerned for each other. I am sovereign and all-knowing. I know all of the needs of the people you bring to Me beyond anything you can be aware of. But I love to hear your prayerful concerns for others expressed to Me. I also delight in answering those particular prayers, for in doing so, the faith of My children who intercede is increased, and they are made even more sensitive to other people's needs."

I felt that I understood better the reason for intercessory prayer. But the Savior had more to say about it, and He continued speaking.

"There is another reason why I desire that you pray for others. In praying for others you take your eyes off yourself. Self-centeredness is a natural characteristic of your fallen nature. When My children are prayerfully concerned for another person's needs, it is a powerful indication that you are entrusting your own needs to Me. I delight when My child is so secure in My love and provision that he can consider someone else's needs before his own."

Before we left the Intercession Bench, I asked, "Lord, sometimes I can't understand certain people, and I find myself critical of them. I know that you would like for me to treat them the way You do me and love them unconditionally. I really want to pray for them, but I have a hard time understanding them and knowing how to treat them. What do I do in a situation like this?"

The Lord replied, "Go to the next area and I will give to you the answer you seek."

SEVEN

The Perspective Place

I continued my walk down the stone path and came upon a pool of water that had collected in the bend of the brook. The pool looked deep but was only about twenty feet wide and thirty feet long. A flat boulder rested on the edge of the water, so I made my way to it and sat down. Then I heard my Savior's voice again.

"This area is called the Perspective Place, for it is here that my children are able to take people whom they do not understand and find wisdom to understand them better. If you will submit yourself to My leadership and seek My perspective on the people that you bring to Me, I will give to you guidance in dealing with them."

I asked, "Lord, what about the people I had mentioned to you . . . would You give me Your perspective?"

The Lord did not reply immediately, so I waited patiently for His answer. Before long, my mind began to recall articles in the newspaper that I had read. Headlines of rape, murder, child abuse, and terrorism floated into my thoughts. Then I saw gangs wreaking havoc in the streets, starving children with sunken eyes, and people chanting with guns raised over their heads. I could not understand why these dreadful images were invading my joyful time in the Sacred Garden. I had to ask, "Savior, why are these terrible images coming to me? What does this have to do with my question?"

"Tell Me what the people in these images are feeling," my Lord replied. "Why is there rage? Why is there cruelty? Why is there fear? Tell Me what the victims are feeling. Tell Me about children in that environment who grow to adulthood. Will they be scarred? Will they be wounded? Will they be cruel? Will they abuse their children like they were abused? Will they have a perspective on life that is different from yours? Do you think that these things will make them hard to be understood by people different from them?"

I knew the answer to the Lord's question immediately. I had never experienced what these people were going through, and I could not understand what their perspective toward life would be as adults. For that reason I could never understand them based on my experience. It would require that my Savior impart to me a sensitivity that could come only from Him. I couldn't require these people to enter my world and do things my way. Instead, I would have to enter their world with the love of Jesus and without a critical spirit, and do things His way.

"Lord, how do I enter the lives of those with such drastic backgrounds? Anyway, most of those people live in different parts of the world and have a different culture. I don't have any opportunity to serve them and I, for sure, have never been critical of those people."

I was looking for a way to justify my lack of involvement and my self-perceived fairness to all people. I didn't know of any people around me like He was showing to me, so I felt comfortable with my excuse.

"My child, open your eyes to what is in your world," the Lord answered.

Immediately, I recalled a near collision that I once had with an old farm truck. The driver had pulled out in front of me as if he was paying no attention to the rest of the traffic. I remembered rolling my window down as I pulled my car next to him and shaking my fist at him. I looked into the cab of the old truck where I saw a family of two adults and three children packed inside. The driver and his wife had tired eyes, and the children were dirty. It was apparent that they were itinerant farm hands who had been working the fields all day and were weary from their work. More than the day's work they had just endured was the life they had to struggle with.

I heard my Savior's voice again, "Tell me what that man was feeling when you shook your fist in his face. Did you teach him anything about driving? Did you feel better about venting your anger? Did it foster anger in his heart toward you and 'your kind'? Tell Me, did your show of fury rob the small amount of self-worth and dignity the poor man clung to? How did he feel as a father and a husband as you rebuked him in front of his family? How did his children feel? Do you think those children will grow up with disrespect for their father and anger toward those that have a better life than theirs?"

The Lord's penetrating questions were being hammered home, and I began to see that I needed much time with Him at the Perspective Place. I felt shame for the critical spirit I had toward people different from me. I felt shame for my lack of empathy and sensitivity. I could see that a lot of my misunderstanding about other people was more my own fault than theirs.

Even though I felt ashamed for my lack of understanding and sensitivity, I didn't feel a harsh rebuke from my Savior, but rather I felt the perspective I was looking for. I felt His teaching and His leadership was leading me from the cultural prejudices and self-centered views I had grown up with to a new view based on His love and mercy. I also made note that this family would be the first on my list when I returned to the Intercession Bench. I was looking forward to having a special prayer time for that family and for the Lord to instruct me how to help them beyond my prayers.

Most of all, I now understood that my world included many opportunities to serve and try to understand those people different from me. My world includes the poor and the wealthy, the humiliated and the arrogant, the down-and-outers and the up-and-outers, and all points in between. I don't have to look far to find them; they are all around me. But I have to look through the eyes of Jesus and not through those of my fallen nature.

The Lord interrupted my thoughts. I was about to ask Him how I could look at people through His eyes and act differently toward them when He said, "The fruits of the Spirit." He then continued, "When you abide with Me, My view and characteristics are imparted to you. You will become sensitive to others and will have the wisdom to relate to them. This will impact the people you come in contact with. In fact, it is the drastic difference I make in your life that will speak louder than words to these people."

"Lord, I have much to learn about life and about You. Where do I find those answers?" I asked.

"Go to the next prayer area for that answer," He replied.

EIGHT

The Meditation Rock

I continued down the path that I had been following and found myself at a large boulder in the curve of the path. The boulder had a flattened area on its top that allowed me a place to sit. I made the short climb to the top of the rock and found a comfortable position to sit while I waited for the Lord to speak to me.

The Lord then spoke. "This is Meditation Rock. I will meet with you here and teach you the meanings and mysteries of Me from My Word. If you really seek understanding, you will find it in My Word. In My Word, you will find all the answers you need for living your life and gaining knowledge about Me. You will also come to understand the life I want for you."

I recalled verses in Proverbs 2:3-6 that spoke of this: "And if you cry out for insight and cry aloud for understanding, and if you look for it as for silver and search for it as hidden treasure, then you will understand the fear of the Lord and find the knowledge of God. For the Lord gives wisdom and from His mouth come knowledge and understanding."

This assurance from my Savior comforted me, for I had always struggled with my understanding of His Word, and I wanted so much to have this treasure opened to me. It was exciting to think that I could ask Him to reveal the truth and the hidden meaning in His Word and He would do it. I couldn't help but wonder, though, if I could trust the impressions that I felt He was giving to me? I know that my feelings alone could deceive me and would be an inconsistent guide, and my feelings could even lead me astray. But as quickly as that thought came to me, another comforting answer was impressed into my thoughts, "All scripture is God-breathed and is useful for teaching, correcting and training in righteousness, so that the man of God may be thoroughly equipped for every good work." I then realized that it was God's Word, not my feelings, that He would use to guide me. I also took comfort in knowing that He promised He would open my mind to understanding, if I would truly seek His wisdom. I decided right then to make my way daily to Meditation Rock for insight and understanding. I was contemplating this thought when my Savior called. I descended the rock I had been sitting on and continued down the stone pathway.

NINE

The Valley of Abundance

The pathway led to a high overlook from where I could see a fertile valley below. As I looked more closely, I could see that the valley was filled with wheat fields, orchards, and all manners of cultivated crops. The crops and fields extended beyond my sight. Surely, this was the most abundant land that I had ever seen. After my initial shock of seeing the valley, I found a comfortable position and continued to enjoy the spectacular view. Before long, I heard my Savior speak to me.

"You are viewing the Valley of Abundance," the Lord stated. "I call it this because it represents the resources that I have at My disposal for meeting all of your personal needs. I want you to trust Me to always meet your needs and to know that it is available for you when you ask for it."

I was reminded of the scripture in Philippians, "And my God will meet all your needs according to His glorious riches in Christ Jesus."

"Savior," I asked, "You have granted me many requests, but several have not been granted. Yet the valley is full. Can You explain why?"

The Lord replied, "Have your needs always been met?"

I thought on His question and I realized that they had. I recalled a few occasions when it seemed my needs had not been granted. However, when it was all said and done, my problems were generally solved with some other solution I hadn't really considered. Before I could answer, the Lord spoke again.

"My child, what do you really know about Me? Can you understand My capacity to see the details of your life and to thoroughly know your total needs? Can you understand My capacity to meet your needs, anytime and anywhere you are? Can you understand One Who is able to create all things and to speak into existence any solution to any problem? Can you see into the future and the problems you might face, if I were to grant a specific request that you make? I can. Can you see the dynamics of how one life affects another and how a specific request granted to one life might hurt another? I can. Now, answer Me this: What do you know about Me?"

I realized this last question was not just for my understanding. A response was required. I answered, "Lord, because of the life Jesus lived out before mankind, I know that You are good and Your love is beyond anything I could understand. I also believe that You love me."

The Lord replied, "Do you trust My love? Do you trust My promises? Do you trust My abilities? Do you trust Me?"

"Yes, Savior, I trust You," I said.

"Then trust Me to provide the right thing for you in meeting your needs," the Lord said. "I will never fail you or never let you down. There will be times when it will appear that I am not responding to your needs, but wait on Me. I am working to meet your need, but in My very special way. Know this: Though I appear to tarry, I will always be right on time. If you will wait patiently for My answer, you will receive a greater blessing than you could have ever realized."

With this last statement from the Lord, I was reminded that Jesus did not immediately respond to the request to go to Lazarus when he was sick. Instead, He allowed him to die and to be buried several days before He showed up at the house of Mary and Martha. Martha was distraught that Jesus didn't get there in time to save Lazarus from death. It was because she could see only one solution to the problem—for Jesus to show up on her timetable and to meet the need with her solution. Jesus had another plan that would bless her and all the people present—a solution that was beyond their wildest dreams. Jesus would bring Lazarus back to life!

This was the point that my Savior was making. He wants to meet more than my perceived needs. He wants to meet what He knows all my needs to be. Martha and Mary needed to have their brother healed and returned to them. But Jesus knew they needed more than Lazarus healed of sickness. Mary and Martha, along with the disciples, needed to know what Jesus was capable of doing. This experience would be essential for their strength, as they soon would watch Jesus go to the cross.

"Yes, my Savior, I trust Your love, I trust Your promises. I trust Your abilities, and I trust You," I stated.

The Lord then said, "My child, you will have other needs you can never see or voice. There will be times when you will be so weary, you won't even voice a prayer. For this reason I have provided for you another special place in My garden. Continue your journey and I will explain it to you when you get there."

Ten

The Shadow of Death

I immediately rose from where I had been sitting and continued down the stone path. The path led down from the mountain and toward the valley I had just been viewing.

The descent into the valley was easy at first. After awhile, though, the path grew more steep and treacherous, and the beautiful flora began to diminish. As I continued toward the valley, the path narrowed and followed a sheer cliff. A trip or misguided step off of the path would surely lead to a fall and to death. My pulse quickened—I've always been afraid of high places—but I continued to follow the path, which finally leveled out and widened. Through willpower and determination, I had made it to safety, and I was feeling good about myself. I walked along quickly and confidently until I came to a blind curve, which I followed around the mountain. Suddenly, the path narrowed to only a few inches. To each side was a sheer drop-off with no shoulder for safety. I looked at the rugged rocks hundreds of feet below, and a cold sweat fell from my brow. I grew dizzy as I looked down.

I don't know what happened to me in my past to make me so frightened of heights. Maybe it's a fear of being totally out of control if I were to fall. Whatever the reason, I had never seen anything so terrifying or so personally challenging as what I was viewing. I looked around but saw no alternative paths. It was apparent that in order for me to continue down the path that God was instructing me to follow, I would have to walk a ridge only a little wider than a tightrope, facing my greatest horror. Every instinct in me cried out, "Don't!" Every intellectual fiber within me pronounced, "Death if you do it!" Every muscle was tense and rigid with fright. I looked back and wondered how I might return to the cottage, but behind me the path led into darkness.

I stood negotiating within myself whether to continue on the path or not, and an angry question found its way to my thoughts. Why did God's Sacred Garden include a frightening place like this? Everything to that point had been so pleasant and peaceful. But this was absolutely dreadful.

"Lord," I cried out, "How can I do this? Why must I do this?"

"Do you trust Me?" was the simple answer I heard.

"Yes, dear Lord, I trust You. But I am so afraid," I replied.

"Follow My voice and I will lead you safely through this threat," He said.

The Lord's voice was calming. As long as I could hear Him speaking to me, I felt courage. But when He was silent, my fear returned.

"Lord," I cried out, "is there no other way?"

"Not if you want the peace and intimacy with Me that you seek," was His reply.

I continued to look at the rocks below and the death that would surely greet me if I followed the path before me.

The Lord said, "Take a step forward and trust Me."

I was at an impasse. To go forward meant death unless God protected me. To not step forward was to continue the spiritual agony that I had been in before entering the Prayer Cottage. It was either to obey my instincts and disobey God or obey God and abandon my instincts.

Although my faith was still immature, I had come to realize that my Savior would do nothing to hurt me, even though my instincts would tell me otherwise. This gave me a measure of comfort. He had proven Himself worthy of my trust and obedience. I continued to assure myself by remembering a phrase I had once heard: "If you have a hard time trusting God's ways, trust His heart. He will never let you down." This was one of those times.

I couldn't understand why He was requiring me to face this frightening choice, but I knew I had to face it. I had to decide if my trust in Him was real or if it was just hopeful.

Humor comes at the strangest times. A slight laugh emerged from my lips as I remembered that just a few steps before, I had patted myself on the back because of my "willpower and determination." There was no amount of determination or willpower within me that would make me take that first step. I was a coward and I knew it. There was no way I could overcome my fear alone. Only one thought empowered me to do it. "Lord, I trust You," were the words I kept saying over and over again.

A thought came to me of how Peter, fixing his eyes on Jesus, defied gravity and walked on water. He must have been frightened by the waves and the sea, but for a brief moment he walked on water. Scripture said that as long as his eyes were fixed on Jesus, he did the impossible. When he began to look at the potential danger and took his eyes off of Jesus, he sank. Even so, Jesus was there holding his hand and keeping him safe.

This was the breakthrough of faith that I was needing. I realized I couldn't do this on my own, but if I fixed my eyes on Jesus, He would hold my hand and get me across to the other side.

My confession of faith to trust my Savior was the act of fixing my eyes upon the Lord. Even though I could not see Him with the eyes of my flesh, when I trusted Him, I could see Him with the eyes of my soul.

I took a deep breath and took the first step. I paused and then took a second step, all along confessing, "Lord, I trust You." As I took these steps, I heard, "Good, My child. Good."

I paused, took another step, and then another. One step at a time, I walked on the precarious path set before me, while my trust in my Savior stayed fixed on Him. I could feel His steadying hand on me as I walked the path.

Like most people who want to get a challenging thing over with as soon as possible, I looked down the narrow path with hopes of seeing it come to an end. But that was too demanding and disappointing, as it seemed to continue indefinitely. Instead, I became content with taking one step at a time and getting assurance from the Lord that I was doing well. As I walked the narrow path, I began to feel more confident, for God's constant assurance kept me steady. Little by little I began to see my greatest fear conquered. I knew it required that I face it, with God's help.

It was strange. When I was finally able to get comfortable with the high place I was in, I began to see beauty like I had never beheld before. The unobstructed view reminded me that I was seeing things that eagles see every day and few humans are privileged to see. A joy fell over me as I began to rejoice and thank my Savior for the privilege of being in such a place with Him! I was astounded. I was actually thanking Him for the challenge that He gave me that caused me to conquer my fear. Most of all, I thanked Him for being with me and keeping me steady. He was walking with me. His complete protection and His trustworthiness were allowing me to do that which had been impossible for me to do before.

As I was praising Him, I was reminded of a verse in Habakkuk. It really hit home with me. "The Lord God is my strength, and He will make my feet as the feet of the deer, and He will make me to walk upon my high places."

I had forgotten my fear. I had forgotten the danger. I had even forgotten about trying to get beyond it. Instead, I was content with His moment-by-moment help with each step I made. In the midst of my praise and contentment, I suddenly realized that the path had widened. There were no more dangerous cliffs to contend with, but rather, a gentle, wide path to the bottom of the mountain now greeted me.

ELEVEN

The Restoration Pool

When I reached the valley floor, I saw an open pasture full of luscious grass. The joy in my heart upon seeing the pasture reminded me of what it must be like for sheep when their shepherd leads them into a new field to feed. In my mind I could see the sheep frolicking in the new grass around their beloved shepherd. I wanted to frolic as well.

As I inspected the new place I had been led to, I could see that the small stream that had originated from the boulder in the Courtyard was now a waterfall cascading over a ledge above me and into the valley. The stream emptied into a pool that was shaded by large trees. I moved closer to the pool and noticed that a mat of grass similar to that in the Courtyard grew around it. The grass was so inviting I could not resist sitting down on it and placing my feet in the cool water. I was tired from my journey, so I lay back and rested my head on the soft grass beneath me. I closed my eyes, drew in a deep breath, and exhaled slowly. As I did so, I started to speak to the Lord. Before I could speak, He interrupted me.

"Remain quiet, My child. Say nothing, right now," the Lord whispered.

I did as the Lord said. After a few moments He spoke again in a hushed tone.

"I call this place where you are resting the Restoration Pool. This is a special place that I have provided My children for receiving My intensive care."

There was a long pause, but it seemed as if His voice continued to linger in my ears long after He spoke. Everything slowed down around me. His lingering words were so soothing, I felt as if I was floating on a cloud. As I continued to lie on the grass with my eyes closed, a gentle breeze brushed over me. My tension left me. My body felt caressed with His loving care for me. Then He spoke again.

"There are times that an extra special assurance and touch from Me is needed by My child. This is the place for that special touch from Me."

It was several minutes before the Lord verbally spoke again. He seemed to be speaking to my heart, my soul, and every cell in my body in a different way. I felt as if I was marinating in His Spirit, and He was imparting to me a special healing that was meeting needs I did not even know I had.

Then the Lord spoke, "You have just completed a demanding journey. At one point on that journey you asked Me why it is necessary for you to face your greatest fear. You now know that it is because I want you to trust Me in the deepest possible way. The process of facing your greatest fears, with Me to help you overcome them, strengthens your trust in Me. My child, I want to bless you by bringing you closer to Me than you've ever been. However, you cannot come closer to me without the abandonment of your fear. You have to learn from your own personal experience with persevering trials that My grace is always sufficient for anything that you face, including your greatest fears. The path that I have just taken you on is called the Shadow of Death. It represents not just your greatest fears, but all of your fears. It also represents your trust or your lack of trust in Me."

I reflected on every word my Savior spoke. He then spoke again.

"You asked why I would include such a perilous journey in My Sacred Garden. Have you considered that My blessings are often to be found in the most unlikely places? Did you not find a blessing in that high place where you were once so afraid? What was the greatest blessing that you discovered? Was it not that I can be trusted? Do you now consider a trial allowed by Me to be a blessing? Do you now understand that My ultimate plan for you is good and best for you? If a trial drives you closer to Me, is that not a blessing? Is that not what My Sacred Garden is about—that you come closer to Me? Yes, My child, indeed, persevering trials are necessary in your journey to Me, and that is why they are part of My Sacred Garden."

There was a long pause before the Lord spoke again. He then continued: "My children will face many kinds of fears and trials that are unique to them. Just as you did with your decision, if my children will abandon their fears to Me and fix their hope on Me to help them, I will help them conquer their anxiety and find a peace that surpasses all understanding. As you have just discovered, with Me at your side, all things are possible for you."

I could now understand the great confidence that is created when we pass through our persevering trials. I was now feeling that there was nothing that I could not face as long as my Savior was with me.

The Lord continued, "This place of restoration is also a special time for Me to minister to you and to restore your soul within you. The journey that you have just been on has challenged your faith, but it has also revealed to you the provision I have provided for the intimacy you seek with Me. You have learned in the Examination Room that you cannot come close to Me with unconfessed sin in your heart. You have now learned that your fears can also stand between us. To come close to me, abandonment of your fears and absolute trust in Me are required."

My eyes continued to remain closed as the Lord spoke to me. I said nothing, but only listened.

He was ministering to me in a way I had never experienced before. Heavenly music filled my ears and found lodging in my soul. A gentle humming anointed me with tranquility and calmness. I felt a warmth move from my head to my toes as the Lord's Spirit moved over me.

As I was basking in this time, I was reminded of the 23rd Psalm. David spoke of the Lord's care being so thorough that he felt he had no needs to be concerned for. He spoke of his Shepherd causing him to lie down in green pastures. He spoke of being led beside still waters. He spoke of being led through the "Valley of the Shadow of Death." He spoke of the comfort he felt because of his Shepherd's rod and staff while going through that valley. He talked of his soul being restored within him.

Before this moment I had thought of this chapter in the Bible as merely a beautiful poem. I now realized that it is a love letter of truth. I, too, was led through my Valley of the Shadow of Death. I, too, was blessed by my Savior's presence and faithfulness during that frightening time. I, too, was led into a green pasture and beside still waters.

Surely I was being bathed in the goodness and mercy of God's love. And I, too, was having my soul restored within me.

"My child," the Savior spoke again, "I said there will be times when you are so weary from your trials that you cannot even voice a prayer. When you come to that time in your life, run to this place and let Me give to you My intensive care. Don't even feel that you have to voice a prayer, for I know your heart and your needs. Just remain quiet. My Spirit will pray for you."

I wanted to speak and ask my Savior to explain better the trials that He was speaking of. As soon as the thought was complete in my mind, He spoke.

"Child, because you are Mine, you will have trials and tribulations. You will be mistreated. I was also mistreated," my Savior said. "I want you to be My champion as you live your life."

I immediately thought of the medieval knights that represented their kings. I thought of how those warriors wore the colors of their kingdom and supposedly represented the king's ideals as they patrolled his kingdom. My thoughts were interrupted when my Savior spoke.

"I want you to take on My characteristics as you learn from Me. I want you to be so closely identified with Me that you become My hands, My feet, My voice, and My love as you influence others to know Me. I want other people to look at you and be reminded of Me. This will bring to you criticism and spiritual challenges as it did with Me when I lived in your world. You will experience wounds because you will be misunderstood, ridiculed, and persecuted as a result of your love for Me. As My champion, you will engage in spiritual warfare, and you will experience spiritual wounds from the enemy. This place is where I bind up your wounds and get you back to the battle. I will meet with you here so I can minister to your needs in the deepest possible way."

After several minutes had passed, the Lord spoke again.

"There are wounds that many of My children endure that keep them from being the men or women that I can make of them. These wounds come from childhood abuse, neglect, or early choices that continue to haunt them. Many of them have no concept of Me as a loving Father, because their own earthly fathers wounded them so deeply. They have a hard time relating to Me on that level. But the truth is, I want to be their Abba, their Daddy, if they will let Me. If they will only trust Me and come to Me for My special assurance, I will never let them down or fail them. If they will come to this place of restoration for My intensive care and let My grace fall over them, as it has you, they will be healed and find the life of joy that they so eagerly desire. They will also find that I am the Abba that their inner being is crying for.

"This special place is also reserved for My child who must bear the burden of the death of a loved one," the Savior continued. "There is no greater grief one must endure than to lose a spouse or a child. I pour out an extra measure of My grace for My child when they come to Me here for My comfort."

I wanted to ask the Lord what I could do to express His love to others and to influence them to come to Him, but again He spoke as if He could read my thoughts.

"When you leave this Sacred Garden, My child, you are entrusted with a sacred duty to be My witness. The best witness that you can be is the way you live your life before other people. Let your actions be inspired by your gratitude to Me and My love for you. Be fair, be merciful, and be gracious. My characteristics are imparted to you as you abide in Me. These 'fruits of the Spirit' are able to affect others as they see how you deal with the difficulties of your life and walk on your high places. These characteristics shine like a light in darkness, and they declare your authenticity. People are attracted to these qualities, for they remind them of Me. However, be very careful not to allow these people to be attracted to you. Always point them to Me. Never put yourself in an intermediary position. Always encourage these people to an intimacy with Me. All My children are given powerful, spiritual ministry gifts that can influence others in a supernatural way. However, they should never use their influence for their own selfish gain. Serve the people I place in your life. Love them to Me, and I will take care of you. You are My champion. Represent Me and My kingdom to your world."

I now had no questions or any words to say. I felt that I understood this place in the Sacred Garden completely, and I felt great joy in knowing that I can always come to this place for that special touch from my Savior in my hour of greatest need.

I also understood that the Prayer Cottage, the Courtyard, and the Sacred Garden, are an invitation to come to My Savior and to enjoy Him. That is something I never realized I could do before entering this sacred time with Him, which is to simply enjoy Him.

I could have lingered in the Garden for as long as the Lord would have permitted, but I started to feel that my time there was complete at that time. I also felt that my life as God's champion was about to begin. I opened my eyes and started to ask my Savior where I go from here. As I did, I realized that I was no longer in the Sacred Garden but had returned to the place where I had begun my journey. I was back on the front porch of the little cabin.

I looked at my watch, thinking that several hours had passed. But I was surprised that only a few minutes had gone by. I had no doubts that the vision given to me was real, for joy and excitement filled my life as never before.

I couldn't wait to get home. Instead of staying any longer, I packed the car and drove home. I had to share with my family what had happened.

TWELVE

Reflection

I left that mountain cabin forever changed. It has been several years since that experience, but I have returned often to the Sacred Garden to find the intimacy with Him that seems to diminish when I get too busy. He always welcomes me back as if I never left. I find something new about my Savior or myself almost every time I visit with Him in the Sacred Garden.

It was difficult at first trying to get back to the Sacred Garden until My Savior showed me how. He instructed me to find a private place, close my eyes, and start my journey in the Grace Room of the Prayer Cottage. After a period of resting in His grace, He would come to me and take me to the Sacred Garden, unless there were issues that need to be cleared up in the Examination Room. Of course, I still have to go the Examination Room from time to time. But like He promised, the more I visit with Him at

Meditation Rock and let Him teach me from His Word, the more I am able to see things that I should avoid.

As I have now made it a priority to spend time with my Savior, I find that it has become an essential part of my life. The more I am with Him, the more I want to linger in the Garden. Most of the time I don't want to leave, but He always urges me to get back to the opportunities that my day will present.

I sometimes wonder what it will be like when I leave this earthen vessel behind. Maybe He will say when I am with Him in the Garden that last time, "My child, the exit to the Sacred Garden is now closed for you. I'm now taking you to the place that you have been longing for in the deepest part of your soul, which is My home. Later I will show you around My universe. Why, I have planets that have waterfalls, mountains, rivers, and oceans that are beyond your wildest imagination. I will show you things that you couldn't conceive of in this lifetime, and it will take you millions of years to see them. Your life with me has only just begun."

I suppose this is why I love being with Him so much. I never get tired of it, and I realize that it is the start of a relationship that will last an eternity. I have much to learn about life and, most of all, about Him. The Prayer Cottage and the Sacred Garden are my school for this. But they are also my refuge. There I find the answers I need for living this life and not wasting the precious investment that my Savior has made in me.

The more I am with my Savior, the more I understand His desire to have an intimate relationship with His children. I even feel His joy when someone finds Him on this level. Sometimes I also feel His disappointment that all of His children do not understand that He wants us to come closer to Him and to enjoy Him. For this reason, I want to champion His cause by telling as many of His children as possible that He is in His Sacred Garden waiting for them to join Him. When I see one of my brothers or sisters make the journey and come back changed like me, I feel His delight.

Perhaps you desire to go to the Sacred Garden. Maybe this is what has been missing in your life and will bring you peace. I know it did for me. I have never been the same since meeting with Him that first day in the Sacred Garden. I hope we will meet and you can share your journey with me after you're back. If not in this life, we can talk about it sometime in the next million years.

EPILOGUE

As the deer pants for the water brooks,
so my soul pants for Thee, O God.
My soul thirsts for God, for the living God.
When shall I come and appear before God?
— Psalm 42:1-2

Does the above verse speak the desire of your heart? Like the Psalmist, are you, too, longing for a deeper intimate time with the Savior? If so, I've got great news for you. God has this same desire for you.

Have you ever thought that what you are actually feeling is the invitation He has given to you to come closer to Him? It's hard to believe, but it is true. The Lord God, Creator of all things, wants to spend special, intimate times with you, so He puts this "thirst" in you that will make you want to drink of His living water. This "living water" is the Lord Himself.

Over the past several years I have seen this thirst for God intensify in His children. Never have I seen it so intense as it is in believers who work in the business world. There is a simple explanation. The business world is full of believers who are being called into a deeper, more intense relationship with our Creator so that we, in turn, can point the way to Him. I believe there is a great awakening within the believers who are in the business culture, and it is from this culture that a great missionary work will be inspired. But reaching the world will not be done with slick PowerPoint presentations and persuasive arguments, the common methods of business. Rather, what will reach the world will be believers who are delighting in their relationship with their Savior and the resulting influence that these lives will have on the people around them.

For the past thirty-four years I have worked within the business culture. The last twenty years I have been privileged to disciple and mentor many men and women who swim every day in the waters of the business world. It is from my experience in this world that I have seen this awakening.

In the discipleship process, I have discovered that it is imperative to encourage men and women to a deeper level of communication with God. Prayer and Bible study are essential tools. Of the two, prayer seems to be the easiest to grasp initially, but the more difficult to go deeper in. Hindrances get in the way, and, as a result, the prayer lives of believers often become unfulfilling and even disappointing. However, for those who break through the hindrances, a whole new world of intimacy with our Lord is opened up before them.

It was in preparation for an extended prayer session with one of my discipleship groups that I wrote the allegorical story you have just read. I was inspired by a prayerful desire to help the participants break through some common obstacles in prayer. The story and a suggested prayer guide were used as preparation tools and directional guides as we separated for our private prayer time. When we came back together, it was with great joy that we all saw great personal breakthroughs and healing. After our debriefing, it was apparent to all that we had been drinking from the Living Water that Christ had been inviting us to.

It is my prayer that you, too, will journey to The Sacred Garden, and you will be able to drink from the well of Living Water that He offers there. May God bless you on your journey.